# JOY IN THE JUMBLE OF LIFE

Joy in the Jumble of Life: 30 Secrets of a Happy Home
By Rebecca Petrie

First edition
January 2015

ISBN: 978-0-578-15654-5 / 0-578-15654-7

Gabriella Press: www.gabriellapress.com
Bulk order pricing available

Editor: Dorothy Leal
Cover: Steve Tyrrell / www.tyrrellcreative.com
Production: Bill Leal

# Contents

## The Most Important Secret

## Secrets of a Happy Marriage

# Secrets of Happy, Secure Children

# *Preface: In Memoriam*

This book is being published posthumously. Rebecca slipped quietly and painlessly away from us in the early morning of 21 January 2014, surrounded by her family. The doctors asked us to leave the room for a few moments. When we returned they had combed her hair and sprinkled pink rose petals all over her bed. There was a bouquet of white Calla Lilies between her hands. What kindness the staff showed to us.

But by far the greatest kindness was the Father's. Because of His love and Jesus' sacrifice she is alive and well, better than she has ever been, in His presence. I've wept with gratitude for His gift of Life to her, and I look forward to our reunion in His presence.

I'm unable to use words like dead, or gone. They aren't accurate. She has just gone on before us, stepped over the horizon beyond where we can see. But she's waiting for us all, and we'll be together again.

With the help of many of Rebecca's care-givers, and the remarkable labor of love by Dorothy Leal, Rebecca finished dictating this book in the autumn of 2013, leaving only editing to be done.

We, Rebecca's family, pray that this book will be a source of insight and life for you. She certainly was that to all of us.

Paul Petrie

# Introduction

"Mom, what are your secrets to creating a happy home?" It was Josefine, my precious daughter-in-law, speaking. She is married to our second son, Phillip. "I imagine following Paul to so many places must have been challenging and at times stressful, yet Phillip's childhood memories are delightful. He often expresses his thankfulness for the happy home that you and Paul created."

What were our secrets? So many thoughts came tumbling into my mind that I could barely express them quickly enough. Josefine grabbed a pen and began to write. As the hours went on, I realized we were creating the skeleton for a new book. So many have asked me to write on other subjects, but none of them seemed right. But as Josefine and I talked together that evening, I got excited for a new project.

This time I am writing to Stephanie, Susannah, Josefine, and Sarah, my three daughters-in-law and my daughter. I will share my heart and open to you our secrets for building a happy home. Hopefully, others will also enjoy these practical evidences of Father's loving presence in the heart of a home. As I look at each of you, my daughters, you are a gift to me, because you are a gift to each son and to Vlatko (you whom I prayed for from the time my girl was a baby—even before I knew your name). In a very special way, you are precious because you are the mothers of my grandchildren.

These are thoughts for each of you in making your home a place of joy in the midst of the pressures of life. I'm thankful to be able to carry you daily to Father's throne, asking that He would give you all that you need to fulfill this calling. My mother always said to me, "Rebecca, there is no higher calling in life than to be a wife and mother, and you have been born into a family of women who are exceptionally good mothers. I know you will be the same."

Thank you, my dears. All my love,

Mom Petrie

P.S. for single parents

It is very helpful and, I think, necessary for you to have a support team around you—a pastor or good friend to whom you can go and keep your life and family open for their input. I remember when my sister Judy's husband died at just forty-six. Judy had four children—from Cathy in her first year of university down to little Tyce who was eight years old.

Soon after her husband's death, Judy left Pittsburgh and moved to Lexington, Kentucky, where Paul and I were able to help her get into a little home for her family. We were able to provide for her a structure that she needed for her life. Paul became and has remained someone to whom she could come and look for counsel.

Through the years that relationship has grown and changed as the children have grown. After my accident, Judy very quickly came to Brussels, and for many years she has been an important part of our support team here. Isn't it a marvelous thing, the tapestry of our lives that Father weaves?

# The Most Important Secret

# SECRET 1

# *Bathe Your Home and Family in Prayer*

I think I have no greater joy than when one of my grown children calls me with a prayer request, asking, "Mama, be sure to pray about that." It's a joy because through the years in our home each one of them learned the importance of Dad and Mom praying for them. Every morning they first went to the family room where they found their dad in his favorite chair, Bible in hand, as he sought the Lord for the day and for each of them. He hugged them and often prayed for their day. Then they came directly downstairs where they found me in my favorite wingback chair with my Bible in hand. There were kisses and good morning greetings, and then they were off to dress and get ready for breakfast.

When our boys got to about thirteen, Paul and I felt that it was time for me to release them from my "mothering" and work more towards becoming friends. Paul took on the principle leadership role in the boys' lives. We felt that my ongoing input to them should mainly be in response to their requests and initiative. So I would ask them, as they left for a special activity or after they expressed a particular need, "Would you like me to pray for you in this situation?"

And I always heard, "Oh, yes, Mama. Please do."

Every morning before they awakened, I pictured each child and held him or her before the Father with praise and thanksgiving, knowing that Father would do His best for them and keep them well. I remember when Phillip took off on his motorcycle for the first time. I was so anxious. My sister, Aunt Judy to them, was with me. We sat on the steps and prayed, committing him to Father. I found out in later years that both Matthew and Phillip had spent a lot more time on those crazy bikes than I ever knew. I guess Father multiplied my prayers, sometimes allowing them a scrape or two to keep them in reality about the danger of their toys.

### My Mother's Prayer List

My mother's faith was the most important part of who she was. After her death, tucked in her Bible, we found a list with many checks in a long line. Someone asked me, "What is this?"

I knew right away. "That is Mother's prayer list. As she prayed for us each day, she made a check." I knew so often that it was her prayers that sustained me. Surely prayer and her relationship with the Lord maintained her joy. Our home was bathed in prayer.

I start with this secret because it is the foundation for all the rest. As wives and mothers, one of our richest responsibilities is in the place of prayer for our husband and children.

# Secrets of

# a Happy

# Marriage

# SECRET 2

## *Guard Your Marriage Relationship above All Others*

When Paul and I married, we understood from the beginning that a home is created by God with the building blocks of the husband and wife cemented together with their love for Him and each other. We were married eight years before we had Matthew. Those were years of conflict and pain and growing. When Matthew came, we were ready to begin to establish the home God called us to.

I remember a later time when Mother visited and witnessed an event that made her say to me, "Be careful to stand with your husband and not with your child against Paul." I knew she was right and, for the very first time, realized that our children could divide us. Our unity as a couple was vital to our children's well-being. We realized that what most gives a child security is not the individual love of each parent for them, but the love of the parents for one another.

Through the years there have been many times when outside pressures have threatened to separate Paul and me. We learned to not let the issue divide us, but to stand together and hold the issue out where we could look at it and discuss the different ways we saw it, and the different ways we were responding to it. Then we'd dialogue about our differences until we arrived at a common approach to the problem.

### Stand By Your Man – in Faith

I remember once walking with Paul. He was so down because of the criticism of wagging tongues against him. I wanted to lash out and defend my man. There's nothing harder for a woman than when her man comes under attack, and she has to stand by and watch the painful process. As we walked that day, hand in hand, suddenly I could see that there would be a turn in the road where we were. My heart was filled with faith, and I could believe for him and the situation.

In the days that followed, when I was confronted by the people who I knew were coming against my beloved, I cried out to the Lord for grace to forgive. My place was to stand in faith, forgiving, and not battling or arguing with the accusers.

There will be many times of pressure from outside and from within that will come against your marriage. In Hebrews 11, we see Sarah's example of faith. It is for all who don't know how to put their faith in action. As women, God calls us to the same, that we would be able to find Him in every situation and bring faith instead of fear. As our men find their destiny in God there will be seasons of testing that will come. At these times it is most important to stand firm together. As Paul has said to me, "Baby, we just have to do this God's way."

# SECRET 3

# *Embrace Your Husband's Calling*

A wife may feel she has understanding or insight about her husband, but she can't begin to do that unless she comes to peace with his calling in God. You can't speak into his life unless you believe in what that life is committed to. It is essential to learn to see your husband's calling as from God.

### The Price of Father's Calling

We waved goodbye at the front door as Paul drove away for a week of meetings. Matt, Susannah, and I walked back inside. Matthew was six and Susannah was three. They were so sad, and I was sad, and I was angry. Why did he have to go for so long? Children this age need their father! Was this the way our life was going to be? I looked down at my little ones, and I could see etched in their faces the same pain that I was feeling. What could I say to them?

Suddenly, it swept over me—whatever my attitude was, they would see it and reflect it in their own little hearts. Anger in me would very quickly turn to bitterness in them. I was frightened, knowing so well that one of a woman's most significant places in the home is a place of influence.

In my heart I turned to the Father. "Lord, help me. Change my heart, change my attitude, and change my mind. Lord, I embrace the pain of Paul being gone. I thank you for his calling. I thank you for the gift that he is to your body. Thank you for the price we have to pay; let your grace help us."

Then words of a similar fashion began to flow to the children: "While Daddy is gone, we will have fun. We will have a very special time, and when he gets home, we will have a party to welcome him." I could see their little faces light up.

Matt said, "I can make a sign that says, 'Welcome, Daddy!' Could we hang it on the front door?" Then Susannah asked if we could make sugar cookies because they're his favorite!

Upon his return, the children were delighted. He always brought little gifts home for each of them on each trip. The children's herd of stuffed animals became huge. Paul would fill us in on his trip with things interesting to the children, then he would give me other details later. All our children embraced his call to travel as a pastor, and ours as a family. We became a team with Daddy.

I learned an important lesson that day. The children would have whatever attitude I had. They were like little sponges, and they would receive many of their attitudes toward life from me. They would feel toward their daddy's travel exactly as I did. There certainly were times during that week that I had to remember my commitment. So we did special activities. We went out for pizza, had lots of their friends come over and did other special activities that helped all our attitudes!

# SECRET 4

# *Women, Learn to Follow in Faith*

Early in our marriage, we traveled all over the eastern United States, sharing and teaching and, outside the meetings, fighting and struggling to understand each other. Paul was learning to lead me and to love me while I was learning to listen to God's leadership through Paul and to follow in faith this wild man that I had married.

Then I began to hear a new teaching: *Wives follow your husband's lead.* I said to Paul, "I've been doing that for years!"

And the Lord responded, No, Rebecca, follow his lead in faith. You just feel you have no option because of Paul's strength. I had, at the same time, become a well-operating manipulator.

Shoofly Pie

One time we were in a lovely home in the southern US state of Georgia. Our hostess had prepared a beautiful meal, and we had eaten well when she brought out a shoofly pie. Now, one of the main areas of conflict between Paul and me was my weight. I had gained weight during the summer before we were married while Paul was away. When he returned I was quite a bit heavier. After we were married, he began to encourage a regimen of dieting. Now you can imagine I was not happy with this plan.

So when our hostess brought out this shoofly pie, under the table Paul laid his hand on my knee as an encouragement not to eat it. But oh, the pie was beautiful. When the hostess asked if we all wanted pie, Paul squeezed my leg tighter. I smiled and said, "Oh, yes, I would like a piece." He squeezed it even tighter. She served me a big piece of pie, and I happily ate the whole thing. My knee was sore, but my tummy was full and happy. I would pay later, but I was prepared.

When we got back to our room, the fight began. We had not yet learned how to navigate disagreements in a way that's consistent with Scripture. That way excludes accusation, harshness, blaming and the use of destructive terms; rather, it includes listening and trying to see the other person's point of view. Instead, Paul was "yelling" at me in whispered tones. I lashed back again in a whisper, even though I knew I shouldn't have had that dessert. We continued, each one struggling for supremacy. While that day I appeared to win, after many encounters similar to this one, I knew I needed to let go of my idol—food. It was my bottom line.

The early years of our marriage were difficult ones. Paul had come from a dysfunctional family. He was strong, and I was strong (and I'm sure Mama was praying). The struggle over my weight became a perfect venue to work out some of these differences. Of course, I was not happy with the weight that I gained, and I found it almost impossible to lose it on my own.

One night after a teaching on *husbands love your wives*, I decided to bring up the conversation of my weight. The insights on husband/wife had been becoming clearer to us, and more implemented in our relationships. Consequently I was experiencing more security in Paul's love and leadership. I opened to him the truth about my weight and the trap that I felt when he'd ask before how much I weighed. I had always lied.

As I shared the reality with him, trusting him in a whole new way, I felt closer and certainly more vulnerable than I had ever been. So you see the struggles over the shoofly pie were just another level of my letting go to follow my husband and the Lord. Over time, the

Lord heard our prayer for a deeper love between us and a stronger foundation and structure for our children to grow in.

# SECRET 5

## *Men, Learn to Lead in Love*

The most important thing in a home is the unity between a husband and wife. Fortunately, in those early years, none of our children were born yet. Meanwhile, as we fought it out, our roles were confused—yet we loved each other desperately. Paul once said of these early years, "I didn't believe in divorce, but I often considered murder."

Then Paul heard the word: *Husbands, love your wives like Jesus loved the church* (Ephesians 5:25). These were words of life, bringing order and structure to our home. Now you know, receiving a word is only the beginning and there are years ahead before it becomes a daily reality.

Slamming on the Brakes:

A Word from Paul

The first time I heard, or at least remember hearing, a Scriptural message on marriage was at a camp in in the late '60s. The words that resonated and rang in my mind were, "Husbands, love your wives as Jesus loved the church." They were not comfortable words. I had spent much more time thinking about Rebecca's responsibility than about my own. The example of His caring leadership clashed strongly with my demanding style.

On the trip home after the camp, Rebecca timidly asked if we could stop at a gas station. This had been a sore topic between us for some years, since my bladder capacity exceeded hers. My idea of stopping on a trip was to fill the gas tank when the light on the dash indicated that the tank was near empty. This was my only motive for stopping. Many fights had ensued from this, as you can imagine.

As I was speeding, probably literally, down the high-way, I heard deep inside a voice I knew: "Paul, would I make the church wait?" I was struck, smitten. We were just coming up to an exit on the highway. I barely had time to exit. I slammed on the brake pedal and took a sharp right onto the exit ramp. Rebecca was shocked—so much so that she later said she nearly wet her pants. That was a turning point for me. I began to think of His kind of leadership more than my kind.

Wow! There are no words for me to express what this change in Paul meant in our relationship. He did not forfeit any of his strength or leadership, but he seemed to see me with new eyes, and I found myself ever growing to be his cherished treasure. We had a long way to go, but Father in His loving grace had put us on the right track, and we began to grow together in leading our home.

# SECRET 6

## *Allow God to Fulfill His Design for You*

This generation has been uniquely affected by influences from without, such as media and technology. An important part of our loss of sexual identity has come through the media. The truth is, in this day and age, it takes a great deal of strength to be a woman of God.

Years ago the Lord gave me a picture that would express how He saw me, and that's how I learned to see myself. It was a beautiful red rose with steel running through its stem. He said to me: "I need you to be a rose with steel in your soul. I created you to be beautiful, both inside and out, and to be strong."

"Good Morning, Mrs. Petrie!"

One day as I drove into the auto repair shop, the mechanic said, "Good morning, Mrs. Petrie." I had now been there so often on my own that even the garage mechanic recognized me and knew my name.

Then the Lord spoke to me: "I've had to work very hard to get you into a place where Paul was not here to take care of you." I knew immediately what he was saying. He wanted me not to be a wimp but to rise up and receive His grace in a hard place with joy. It was soon after that that the Lord showed me the image of the rose. And every time I felt an experience stretching me where I didn't want to be stretched, I knew Father was putting steel in my stem.

God's design is to have family be the core, the building block of society. Every block of society must have a leadership structure. So he fitted man to lead. At a very early stage in the womb, male babies are fitted for the challenges of leadership in a wash of testosterone that separates the two spheres of the brain, allowing a man to make rational decisions without the dominance of the emotional side and to make difficult decisions in rational ways (see for example the Baby Center's report at: http://tinyurl.com/pwto8lr). In a way that a woman can't, a man can go to war and fight with disregard for his safety, being committed to the goal of defending his country, regardless of personal cost. A woman would be thinking of her children, her family responsibilities and needing to be protective of her life for their sake. It's a remarkable God-given distinction, for social purposes.

Little girl babies remain without that separation. The testosterone in boys decreases until puberty and then again increases. I believe it is because Father designed it so little boys will be able to be affected and taught by their moms as well as their dads in the early years. A woman relates to life as a whole. She is made for nurturing. As our husbands lead through life, we are to follow full of faith. A woman's true strength comes from her faith. Early on, as I sought God for clarity and understanding in all of this, I happened to be reading in Hebrews 11 where it lists the people of faith throughout Scripture, including Sarah: "Because Sarah had faith, she was able to have a child long after she was past the age to have children. She had faith to believe that God would do what He promised. Abraham was too old to have children. But from this one man came a family with as many as the stars in the sky and as many as the sand by the sea." (Hebrews 11:11-12 NKJV)

Following another's lead is often misconstrued as being a wimp and not strong. Sarah's strength was the strength of God. It came to her through her faith. I realized God was calling me to Himself to a life of faith, and, in that way, I would become the strong woman God needed to follow my husband.

# SECRET 7

# *Journey with Father to Find Your Uniqueness*

Sarah, my son Stephen's wife, has asked, "How do I be my best true self? How do I define what's important to me?" For me it has been a journey discovering these realities. I have never taken a journey alone. It always begins with Father and my beloved Paul. On this unfolding journey I have discovered who I am, my true self, my uniqueness, and what is really important to me. But it is always an ongoing process.

## 300 Pounds, but Who's Counting?

You need to know that I've not always included Paul in every aspect of my journey. The result of that was, of course, a distance between us. I believe, for me, finding my true self, my uniqueness, my identity, was tied up in Paul and this recognition. I had an idea of who I was, but it was twisted and fuzzy.

One example, as I've mentioned, had to do with my weight. Paul had a vision for me to be attractive and healthy (of course, that's the way he likes me). He saw me, I realized later, as God saw me. We fought and struggled over this many times before I finally came to that realization. And now these days I'm a quadriplegic and have little control over my weight or my figure. Amazingly, the Lord has given Paul grace so that he enjoys his rounder wife as much as he did when I was slim.

This story portrays an area of my journey over the years in finding my true self. The journey begins with Father but must include a journey not just by myself but with Paul. My two companions in every journey are the Lord and my beloved. It may be a simple matter of years. Paul and I married when we were twenty-one, and now we are sixty-eight. We have spent most of our lives together. So, you see, Father and Paul help define my uniqueness and identity.

# SECRET 8

## *Find Your Calling in God*

Early on Paul and I realized that as surely as he was anointed for a task in God, so was I. I was blessed in Paul's determination that my gifts in God were as important as his and needed to be fulfilled. I think his encouragement enabled me to find out and know who I was and what God was calling me to do. It also put in me a deep desire to make Paul's call my first priority. I believe this balance is key. It's the key to finding yourself and begins with you making a choice—a choice to follow your husband and serve him while expressing honestly your own desires and needs as well as what you feel God is saying.

Just this morning Paul said, "We've got to have lunch together today. We have guests in the house, but I've hardly seen you for a week. And we have things that we need to talk about." I knew what he meant. He was facing important decisions and choices that he had to make about his coming schedule and ministry, and he needed to hear my perspective. What a joy it is to me (at sixty-eight!) that he knows how important my ear turned toward the Lord is to him.

### Can I Change Your Job Description?

I had dropped Paul off at the train station with a member of Parliament who had spent the night with us. The men were off to Strasbourg and the meeting of Parliament there. As I came to a red light, I was furious. I cried out to the Lord, "Father, you never called me to this! You called me to women. You called me to my children and my home. You never called me to this! You never called me to government officials and the political realm."

The Lord spoke: "Can I change your job description?"

Paul had just begun a new outreach into the European Parliament, and, as always, I would be included. Our life was already full. Matthew and Susannah were grown and gone from home, but the little boys were still very much there. I was involved in ministry to women, and my heart was at home with my children. I could feel the stretching. I could feel the demand once again of expanding my soul to include yet another world.

In every situation I found the beginnings to be the most difficult, probably because of the resistance in my own heart. As I let go and allowed God to change my heart and mind and give me His, things became easier, and I was able to follow with grace and joy, able to find my true calling and give it to the purpose of God.

# SECRET 9

# *Find Hidden Treasure in*

# *Obedience*

Sometimes we women find a special treasure for our family and ourselves when we obey our husbands against what we feel. A perfect example is described in this next story, of one of many instances. Oftentimes Father has a treasure for us that we are not willing to see or hear. He will speak it to our husbands so that He can give it to us through them.

### The Treasure of Obedience

"I just can't do it. Maybe you have no idea what you're asking me. If I have my quiet time in the morning and get cereal bowls and boxes on the table and lunches made for the boys and Susannah, I'm doing very well." I expressed myself fully and with no small amount of emotion.

Paul looked at me and sternly said, "Baby, I want you to set the table and make a cooked breakfast every morning for these children. I have very little regular time with them. As Susannah has gotten older, she often has activities during the dinner hour. Breakfast is the only time we can be sure to have them all together. We need the order and the reason for the children to want to come. Pancakes or eggs and toast will do it. It will be a peaceful time for me to have our family together."

For about two weeks I cooked breakfast, but it was only out of obedience. Finally in my quiet time one morning, the Lord spoke to me and said: "You know, Paul is obeying me." By the omission of any mention of me I understood clearly the implication that I had not been obeying, only doing. I repented and thanked Him. That morning I had a shorter quiet time. I reminded the Lord that I would obey. I set the table, and by the time I had scrambled eggs, I had a thankful heart. Each piece of toast was covered in thankfulness.

The next morning I had another idea—I could set the table the night before. As I set the breakfast table that evening, there began to bubble a joy in my heart. By the end of the week, my husband and I were serving our children the Word with their breakfast.

I recently heard "grace" defined as "God doing in me what I can never do myself." I was always looking for ways to broaden and deepen our family experience and give gifts to the children. Through this story I can see both happen. I felt my plate was already full. I could add nothing more, but Father knew I had plenty of space and more to give. I only had to open my heart and let him change my mind and give me His perspective and grace.

# SECRET 10

# *See Your Husband through God's Eyes*

Conflict will arise when a man is gone on a trip for a week or two—or even a month or longer. He arrives home exhausted. He's been eating out every night and just wants to eat at home and watch television. Meanwhile, I have been home with children and am ready to get a babysitter and go out to a restaurant for a quiet dinner together.

For years I had complained to Father because Paul traveled so much and, it seemed, every time he was away something happened. The car broke down, a child became ill, or the furnace stopped working in the middle of winter. All of these catastrophes were mine to deal with alone. I complained to the Lord that I might as well not have a husband. I might as well be a single mother. I knew better than that, but I felt the strain and stress of having to deal with crises alone. Why couldn't these things happen when Paul was there, because he would have taken care of them gladly? It was into this context that Father spoke about the privilege of serving my husband.

## A Hidden Privilege

I had been home with three children. Phillip Paul was just a baby, Susannah was about nine, and Matthew, eleven. Paul had been traveling and came home to a special meal and a great welcome home. He went immediately to his office to prepare for the coming week. The children and I cleaned up the dishes, and I got them ready to go to the Sunday evening church service. Paul came down just in time to go and looked at me. "Baby, you look exhausted," he said. "You need to stay home tonight. Let me take these three children, and you stay here and rest." My heart soared. How kind of him and oh, to be free to stay home by myself!

They all packed in the car and drove out the driveway. I turned to realize that the house was a wreck, and I began by doing the dishes and getting the kitchen all cleaned up. Then, in the dining room, the children's toys had been left everywhere. After cleaning them up along with picking up the Sunday newspapers, I finally made my way upstairs where all I wanted to do was lie down and rest.

Upon opening our bedroom door, I discovered Paul's suitcase lying open on the floor. He had just returned from a trip. It all had to be put away. I wanted to say bad words as I hung up his clothes. Finally, I picked up his shoes, and, by this time, I was furious with him. What had begun as a sweet gift had turned sour. I took his dress shoes and threw them into the bottom of his closet. As they clunked, suddenly the Lord spoke: "It is a privilege to serve a man of God."

That evening was another turning point in my relationship with Paul. I knew now how Father saw my husband. I'd been praying to see him as God sees him. I had never considered that God saw Paul with eyes different from mine. I had respected him, but from that night there was a new degree of honoring my husband. That doesn't mean I always remembered, but I had it underneath now, well-hidden in my heart.

# SECRET 11

# *Choose Priorities Wisely and Carefully*

Our culture today has called women out of the home and into the work place. One example of this is my physical therapist, who works with me five days a week. She has been a gift to me and a major factor in restoring my life and movement after my accident. We've become good friends, and I have been with her through many changes and adjustments in her personal life. When we first began, Donatienne was enormous and pregnant carrying twins. It was just the beginning of her burgeoning family, which, in the coming years, would grow quickly to include five adorable, active, delightful children.

They love to come and visit me. Each time they ask again about my accident, why I ride in a wheel chair, and even say, "What kind of candy do you have today?" An older one, rebuking the little one, says "It's not polite to ask." But they know a visit to me is always accompanied by sweets.

Donatienne has made difficult and, I believe, wise choices. Like so many women in our Western culture, she has been pressed into the work place. This choice is made easier when we are able to release our children into Father's hands and then do what He has given us to do. We too must make wise choices.

### His Grace Is Sufficient

I felt like my heart would break as once again I was leaving my precious children. This time we were going for a special group of meetings to Saskatchewan, Canada. It was a Bible school. We had become quite a team, Paul and I. He would teach from the Word, and I would follow, sharing our life experiences. The Lord blessed our time together and blessed the Word and this sharing in an unusual way.

I looked trim and quite smashing in my dusty pink corduroy pant suit. Little did I know the airline would lose our luggage, and I would wear it every day until the students in this school took pity on me and put together a fresh wardrobe of their own clothes. Our luggage was not returned to us for about six months.

In one meeting while Paul was teaching, my heart ached to be home with my children. I opened my Bible to

Psalm 84:3: "Even the sparrow has found a home, and the swallow a nest for herself, where she may have her young—a place near your altar, LORD Almighty, my King and my God". Here the Psalmist talks about laying her treasure, her young, on the altar and leaving it in God's hands. Suddenly, I saw my treasure, and I began to weep and lay them on the altar, safe in Father's hands. The letting go and acceptance of the price of what God had called us to was the release my heart really had been looking for.

The treasure is releasing our children and leaving them in Father's hands. That releasing begins when they are little and goes on throughout their whole lives, even when they are adults. There are demands on women of our day that are unique. In some ways I feel it is a well-constructed plan of the enemy to destroy the home. Each family must find their way through to be able to maintain their home with Biblical underpinnings and faith.

Learning to release our children, with faith in the Father's faithfulness to them, as well as to us, is such an important lesson. God is our first priority. We make the choices of our lives and our schedules, by following the leading of God, not by holding protectively to our own or our children's lives. He teaches us and leads us to live a life of release, and of faith. Each family must determine the Father's plan for them and His call on them, and then choose His plan in confidence that He will oversee the process. Making wise decisions is a process of faith.

# SECRET 12

# *Find Strength in God in Times of Emotional Weakness*

When life or our husbands give us more than we feel we can bear, we must learn to run to Him. When I was younger I found it very difficult to let go of what I felt, partly because those feelings were my protection. If I didn't think I was able to do something, then I felt that I didn't need to do it.

### Hiding in My Feelings

"I just can't do it! It's just too much. I don't know what you think I am made of. I'm losing it." Paul and I were sitting on the couch in the living room. He had just gone over our proposed schedule for the next week. From the start of our relationship, we knew that our ministry included an open home. Besides our four children, we always had someone in need whom we had invited to live with us. For me, maintaining the house and the children was about all I was able to do, and here he was proposing dinner guests four nights this week. I cried and I grew angry—tactics that usually turned the tide.

But Paul stood firm. "You know, Baby, you are using most of your energy in resisting. I suggest that you rather reach to Him for faith to do His will. I'm sorry but I really feel this entertaining is necessary right now."

I knew he was right, and in turning my heart from my weakness to Father's grace, I heard Him say: "My strength is made perfect in weakness." Indeed it was an opportunity to prove His Word.

We often find ourselves in difficult situations, such as this example above, which demand more of us than we feel willing to give. Oftentimes Father asks us to make difficult choices, to choose against ourselves and to choose for our husbands. Only Father's grace can enable us to choose against ourselves for the advancement of His kingdom and purposes.

# SECRET 13

# *Manage Hormones and Their Effect on Family*

It's a very difficult thing for a man to know the raging emotions that can be in his wife during her monthly cycles. It is important for us women to express the emotions going on during that time of the month. Open communication around this subject can provide a wonderful opportunity for mutual sharing and understanding.

Father made man and woman so very different. During her cycle and pregnancy a woman experiences such a wide range of emotion, and a man has no way to understand unless we be able to express to them what's happening inside. It's so important, as Father opens up opportunities, that we are able to express to one another what's happening within.

If we don't communicate, there's no way to understand each other. The unfolding of this process takes time and opportunities to communicate. It's an important part of a woman's place to pray for these opportunities and to wait on the Lord for Him to provide the perfect time to communicate her heart to her husband.

## You Think I'm Acting Badly?

"You think I'm acting badly? What I'd like to do is pick up every chair in this room and throw them through the window! Now that would be acting badly." I was expressing to Paul my feeling during my period. That day he had been communicating to me how badly I was acting and how I needed to control myself and not just act out what I was feeling. It was the perfect opportunity to express to him what I really felt. I was actually controlling myself very well. He looked at me in amazement. Through discussions like this he began to get a glimmer of what it was like to be a woman in the midst of her cycle.

I remember another time when we were at Christ Center in Lexington, Kentucky, and the men had been encouraging us as women of God to wear long skirts and dress in a modest fashion. After about a week of wearing these skirts, I said to him, "You know what I think of you and your long skirts?" At this point I took off the skirt and began to kick it all around the room and then proceeded to jump up and down on it.

He looked at me in utter amazement and said, "Yes, sir, that's my godly wife." At this point we looked at each other and laughed, realizing that we were beginning to understand each other and that I was beginning to express myself and let him know the reality of our differences.

It is vital to learn to wait on God's timing for the opportunity to communicate important things about ourselves and our needs to our husbands. Father will provide the perfect time for such communication. When I want to scream and demand, that is a sure sign that I need to wait on Him in faith. It must come in His timing and not be demanded by my need.

# SECRET 14

# *Trust Your Husband to Discipline with Love*

In the area of child training and discipline, perhaps more than any other, the differences between a man and a woman are evident. Some-one has said that a woman carries a child for nine months close to her heart and so looks at that child in a different way than her husband does. This is a part of God's plan and why it is so important for us as women to have a man's perspective in the area of discipline.

A man may be able to be more objective and see the situation as it really is. He is usually able to administer discipline firmly and with authority. But that's the way God did it. A child instinctively knows that it's a perfect plan when the husband and wife are in harmony and working together. One is able to bear the weight of the discipline while the other is ready to love and comfort. It is very important for the child's sake that these two be in one accord.

## Jump into Daddy's Arms

Phillip had been playing on the bed of a huge Mack truck which was parked in the hangar on the mission station in the Congo. We had traveled in Congo many times through the years. This visit was one of the first times our three-year-old son Phillip came along. He was delighted with the wide open spaces to run and play with the other children on this mission station.

Paul came to the back of the truck and said, "Phillip, jump to me. Jump into Daddy's arms." Phillip timidly came to the edge of the truck and suddenly realized how very high he was and sternly refused his dad's request. After several requests, Paul took him down quietly and lovingly disciplined him, explaining that he needed to obey his daddy's word.

Once again, Phillip was back up on the truck bed. Paul said, "Now, Phillip, jump to me!"

Phillip began to cry. "No, Daddy, it's too high." Paul took him down, disciplined him again, and returned him to the truck bed.

"Phillip, jump to me." I'm not sure how long this process continued, but in the end an obedient little boy, with a tear-streaked face, jumped into his daddy's arms.

You can imagine the differences in Paul's and my response. When Phillip finally committed himself to his father's arms, Paul held him, loved him, and said, "Son, sometimes we are all afraid. But we mustn't let fear control us. We must always do the right thing even when we are afraid. We must be able to overcome fear when it hinders us from follow God and His ways."

Phillip looks back on this memory with fondness and thankfulness. He says this was a turning point in his life—an important step in becoming the strong man of God he was created to be.

For me, this day was another real turning point. It was a lovely opportunity to see my husband's training through God's eyes. We were different, but neither one of us was wrong. God had made us as we were for the forming and maturing of each of our precious children.

Once again, single parents may find discipline hard and may need to be encouraged by the support people in their lives, particularly the male support person and his wife. I remember how often Judy called to talk with Paul or me about the children and received clarity and courage through Paul's words and insight.

# Secrets of

# Happy, Secure

# Children

# SECRET 15

## *Create a Secure Structure*

A happy home begins with structure. There are two types of structure. One is a home with a father and mother. The other, from the experience of my childhood with a widowed mother, is a home with a single parent being both dad and mom for the children.

My father was killed in an automobile accident when I was five years old. Almost immediately my mother began working. We came home from school for lunch every day, and I can still see Mama walking up the hill toward home as I descended from school. We walked in the lane together, discussing what we would have for lunch. Three of my older sisters were already married, so only my older sister Judy and I were at home. Mom had never had to work, so plunging into the business world must have been a terrible shock to her. Her pain and loneliness at having daddy taken so suddenly was surely terrible, but she never allowed her mourning to darken our home.

Later, she told me she realized she had to go on because of Judy and me. She had to create an atmosphere where we could grow. She was the mother, and, in order for me to remain the child and be allowed to grow as God intended, she had to maintain her role as both mother and father.

I cannot begin to express how well she did. She disciplined me when I needed it. She trained me and always loved me. No matter how difficult things might have been at school, I always knew my mother was on my side. I remember she always spoke the truth to me. Her wisdom became a bulwark around me, insuring my security. I have a picture of her in her later years. We had it framed and beautifully mounted, and I love it, especially because it catches the twinkle in her eye. Mama taught us, no matter how difficult and dark a situation might be, always to look for some positive side about it. Our life at home was joyful and full of sparkle.

As a single mom probably the most difficult thing for her was discipline. I was not a difficult child. I know that helped her a lot. But I do remember a few times when I did need discipline.

## Mama vs. Roy Rogers

One Saturday afternoon I had done the dishes and went hurrying off to the movies. Instead of finishing my job by drying and putting them away, I left them in the draining rack. I had to hurry as I was going to miss the opening of my Roy Rogers movie. I cannot tell how mortified I was that, while I was watching the movie, my little mother came and pulled me out of the theater to come home and finish the job I had left.

Most of the discipline I needed had to do with my work in the house. Every Saturday morning I had the responsibility of scrubbing the upstairs bathroom and the stairs down to the living room. Many a week I did the same job at least two or three times until I got it right. As I write these stories others flood to mind but let me write just one more.

## A Pinch under the Arms

It was Sunday morning, and we were sitting in our normal pew, second from the front in the Methodist church. The preacher was an older man, and it was communion Sunday. As he held the bread, the napkin drooping over the edge, unknown to him, dipped into the grape juice below. It acted as a wick, and the cloth became increasingly purple. Well, to the two young girls in the pew, it was hilarious, and we started to laugh.

Mother looked at us with a disapproving scowl. Our laughter could not be thus contained. Mother at this point reached over and pinched each of us as hard as she could under the arm to make us be serious. It was not very effective and made us laugh even harder. Even though we tried to hold it in, we laughed so hard that we shook the entire pew! Although she couldn't admit it there, later around the lunch table Mom admitted she was giggling on the inside, too.

Mother was four feet and eleven inches, a single mom, raising two daughters by herself. Yet she kept good discipline in our home and created clear boundaries, maintaining all that we needed for a secure, stable, and happy atmosphere to grow in.

# SECRET 16

# *Learn to Hear Your Children's Hearts*

There were many factors of our home that were unusual because of the nature of Paul's ministry. For many years, we maintained two homes, one in Lexington, Kentucky, where we spent the summers for Paul to work in North America, and a rental in Brussels, where we flew at the end of August. How do you maintain a secure family structure in these circumstances? Somehow we managed—in part by learning to hear our children's hearts. And what joy that can bring us as well.

### Learning to Hear Susannah's Heart

One day when we had just arrived back in the states, someone said to Susannah, "Susannah, which is home: Lexington or Brussels?"

I held my breath, wondering what in the world this six-year-old child would say. She thought for a moment, then smiled and said, "Home is wherever Daddy and Mommy are." Well expressed, my precious girl!

While our situations may not be perfect, and our relationships the same, as long as our focus is clear and we are working toward oneness of heart in our marriage, the Lord will create the structure for our children to grow. And we will learn to hear their hearts and His heart in them.

Into this context it's important that we learn to listen carefully to our children's hearts and not to laugh and make fun of things they say or do, even when it's cute to our adult ears.

### That's Not My Name

When I got home, coming in the front door from running errands, Susannah greeted me, laughing while she gave me the news, "Mom, Tooty has run away from home, but I doubt he's gone far. He left a note. Wait until you see it. It's a real crack-up."

Sure enough, there on the kitchen counter in his precious first grade scrawl was the note: "Mom, I have run away from home. My name is not Tooty. My name is Stephen!" We both laughed, confident he hadn't gone far.

I realized there was something deeper in his scrawled little note. "Lord, let me see and hear this little boy."

Susannah asked, "Mom, should I go looking for him, or shall we just wait until he's tired of hiding?"

"Perhaps a little of both," I replied. I went to the front door and called, "Stephen!" I was using his real name, not "Tooty," although it was a little sad in my mother's heart that my baby had given up his nickname.

After about an hour Susannah said, "Mom, I think he's under the front bushes." I went out looking to the left and the right, and there he was in his hiding place, very obvious, as he wanted to be found. Later, he told us of his adventure of running away from home. He had run away almost a full block and hidden under a small bridge. He hid there, but realizing he couldn't be found, moved closer to the house under the front bushes.

Stephen was our fourth child and definitely my baby. I realized that day that running away was one of his first demands to grow up. From the time Stephen was born, Phillip, his older brother by three years, could not say his name, and thus he became "Tooty." We all thought it was cute, and so everyone called him "Little Tooty." This is a perfect example of learning to listen to little voices.

Stephen had said he didn't like to be called "Tooty," and we might for a day or two comply, but inevitably we slipped back into calling him his baby name. It was a funny story, his running away, but we all knew that his heart was crying out and demanding his clear identity. One day soon after, Paul made a decree for the whole household that Tooty's name was Stephen. And so it was from that day onward.

# SECRET 17

# *Create Surprises and Celebrations as a Center for Life Together*

Early in our relationship, we realized that Paul was the manager and director of our home, but I was the creative force that helped bring life and joy into the atmosphere. Paul gave me *carte blanche*, saying, "You need to be the activity director for this ship." We began to set forth the programs that would create fun for our life together by creating special memories and times for our children. Always be aware that life is a celebration, and a celebration often bursts into a party. We had many different celebrations in our family.

**The Great Outdoors: Celebrating God's Creation.** Hikes and walks were always important, and it is very special to children to have some kind of a picnic along the way. I remember in California, we would hike up into the hills around San Jose. In those days, there were no restrictions regarding building a fire. We would build us a little fire and cook hot dogs to eat for dinner. What fun, and what an adventure for little ones! When the children got older and could run and explore, it provided quiet moments for Paul and me. Also, older children often want to bring a friend along, and occasionally we became a much larger group.

Hikes and nature walks can happen any time of year. In the spring to explore and find all the plants and trees and signs of new life was the challenge. In winter to build a fire to warm us was very special. In fall, of course, we loved to collect beautiful leaves. We would bring them home and iron them between sheets of wax paper. Those waxed leaves make beautiful books and are a great reminder of our walks in the autumn.

Just before we began work on editing this part of the book, I received a call from Susannah to tell me about Marta's first day of preschool. Suddenly she realized she had the entire morning free with just the little boys. She tucked Nikola into the snuggle sack and put Filip into a stroller, tied on his little red cap and fall jacket, and off they went for a nature walk. What fun for them to have a special time with mama alone, collecting leaves, berries and, of course, very special rocks. When they came home, they made their first album of collected treasures of their walk together.

**Birthdays.** It was early in the morning on Matthew's 7th birthday. Paul and I sneaked quietly into his room and sat on the end of his bed. "Happy birthday to you ...." His birthday song was sung for the first of many times that day. When we came downstairs, the breakfast room table was set with a gift at Matthew's place, and the smell of pancakes, his favorite breakfast, was in the air. So we began the special day to celebrate our first-born son. We felt it was important for each child to have the opportunity to be the most important person for their day. This time it was a day to celebrate Matt.

Each birthday was different. Some years there were special parties with the children's friends. I remember Susannah's "Little House on the Prairie" party, and how all the children came dressed in little prairie dresses. For this birthday, we were eating so carefully without sugar, so I made Susannah a whole-wheat and honey birthday cake. It looked beautiful, but it tasted so bad that not one of the children would even eat past their first bite. "Momma, please, please, don't ever bake me a birthday cake again."

**Un-birthdays!** We had an Alice in Wonderland book. When Alice and the Mad Hatter had a party, we decided we could have a party too! In the book, they had a pink tablecloth. Matt said, "Mom, we must have a pink tablecloth!"

The next day, Paul and I were going out to lunch. It was our weekly celebration of our love and life together. It also gave us time to talk without the children. After lunch, I told Paul I needed to stop by a linen store, as I had a very special tablecloth I was looking for. He was quite surprised when I chose a bright pink, square cloth. But when I explained, he was more than happy to buy it for us. Coming home, the children saw it and were delighted. It was exactly like Alice's cloth in the book. So we were off.... I used my nicest tea pot and china, and we learned the song from the record that had accompanied the book: "A very merry un-birthday to you, to you, a very merry un-birthday to you, to you, a very merry un-birthday to you, and it might as well be you, a very merry un-birthday to you." Daddy was invited to that very first un-birthday party. We could have an un-birthday party anytime for anyone.

I remember one un-birthday celebration in particular. Uncle Frank and Aunt Millie Dawson were coming from the United States. The pink tablecloth and tea things were all arranged, and it was decided—it would be Aunt Millie's un-birthday. When they arrived, we began to sing, and much to their surprise, the party began!

**New Season Celebrations.** There were celebrations for the beginning of seasons, and certainly a celebration for the first snowfall. When they were teenagers, I remember one of those snow days. I believe Phillip was a baby. We turned the couch around to face the French doors, put a blazing fire in the fireplace, and sat on the couch there in the den. We drank hot chocolate and watched the snow pile up in the garden outside. All of this gave an air of excitement to our lives together.

**Create Special Times with Each Child.** There's nothing that makes our children feel more special than alone time with Dad or Mom. When Susannah was a senior in high school, I felt a needed to secure her anchor to her daddy and me. It came to me to create a special half day together. I wrote a note asking for Susannah to have Wednesday morning off as we had a "family need." Keeping my precious daughter close was certainly a need under any circumstance! What fun she thought it was. Susannah said later, "Frankly a Saturday together would have been great, but getting out of school for half a day to be together was really fun!"

# SECRET 18

# *Build Traditions at Christmas*

On Christmas Eve the youngest child in our family has the special joy of plowing into the pile of gifts under the tree and one by one placing them at the feet of their owners. The excitement builds as each child waits to see who has the most! Oh, dear, will we be able to sleep tonight when we see what treasures we have to open in the morning?

### Oops, We Let the Cat Out of the Box!!!!

One Christmas was especially memorable. This Christmas Susannah got to open the first one even though she wasn't the youngest. But hers was the most difficult to contain. "Quick! Paul, stick it in the box and tie the ribbon." Then, "Come on, children, you may come down." The children stood waiting on the stairs until we gave them the OK to come and join us at the Christmas tree. At this point, we handed Susannah the large box with the big red bow. There were scratching and growling sounds from within. She timidly untied the ribbon and peeked in. "MEOW!! "

Feeling the joy of liberty, the grey tabby cat came bounding out of the box, and Susannah shrieked with joy. But Hazel, like a gray and black streak, went up to the top of the Christmas tree. The tree swirled and swayed, and ornaments flew. She hung from the top with the angel, yowling and squawking from her high perch. As Paul looked at me, the children squealed with delight. Paul said, "We might have a problem here." That was just the beginning of our life with Hazel.

Hazel and I soon developed a daily ritual. I would sit in the wingback chair early in the morning and have my quiet time. Every morning Hazel came purring around my feet, and I poured her some milk in my saucer. Then one day she ate my canary and I was mad! The morning after she ate my canary, she came purring around my feet, but I was still furious: "You eat my canary one day and expect me to give you milk the next!"

The Lord broke through and quietly said: "How many times has you eaten my canaries and not treasured what I treasure?" I humbly poured the milk in the saucer, forgiving Hazel as He had so often forgiven me.

When the gifts are settled around the tree, Paul and I head off to bed. As Christmas dawns, the children awaken us with their wild anticipation. Paul groans to me, "Baby, I'll be so glad when they grow up, and we can all sleep in on Christmas morning." As it is, we head downstairs, and everyone sits behind their piles. But the first thing— the most important thing—Daddy picks up our special book and begins to read. When the story is finally finished (at least, that's the feeling of the littlest ones), it's time to open the gifts. The story that Daddy always read is a wonderful pop-up book by Hallmark called *The Christmas Story*. Here is a summary.

### The Very First Christmas

Over 2000 years ago a great emperor ruled much of the world. He ordered that a tax be collected from everyone who lived in his lands. Each person had to go and pay their tax in the city where he was born.

At this time there was a carpenter named Joseph who lived in the town of Nazareth. He was not happy about this tax because it meant he would have to make the long trip to Bethlehem where he had been born. He was especially worried about his young wife Mary. She was soon going to have her first baby. But they didn't have a choice. They had to go. So Joseph helped Mary get on their donkey to make the long trip. He was careful to stop and rest often.

They must have talked of many wonderful things on the trip, like the angel who came to tell Mary she was specially chosen to be the mother of God's Son. Another angel had told Joseph they were to name him Jesus, which means Savior, because Jesus would save everyone from sin. Even though Mary was tired, she must have been very happy waiting for the baby to be born and to hold him in her arms.

When they came to Bethlehem, they couldn't find a place to spend the night. It was getting dark. At last they came to the last hotel in Bethlehem. The innkeeper was sad to turn them away, seeing how tired Mary was, and how pregnant. So he offered to let them stay in the stable where there was fresh, clean hay. They could lie down and rest there. Mary knew the baby would soon be born, so that is where they stayed.

On the same night in the fields outside Bethlehem, a group of shepherds were watching their sheep in the fields. Suddenly a very bright light pierced the dark sky.

The shepherds were frightened and confused and fell to the ground. Then an angel of God appeared to them and said, "Don't be afraid, for I bring you good news of great joy." The angel told them how the Savior of the world was going to be born that very night in Bethlehem. They were to go and find him lying in a manger in a stable!

In the stable, Joseph made a bed of straw for Mary. There, surrounded by the animals, Jesus, the Son of God was born. Mary must have wept tears of joy and love to hold her little boy close to her heart. He was small and beautiful. Joseph helped, and carefully wrapped the child in the clothes they had brought for him, and then they laid him in the manger filled with fresh, sweet hay.

Later that night the shepherds found their way to the stable the angel had talked about. They were so excited as they gathered around for a close look at baby Jesus. Their hearts must have burst with joy!

After some time, three wise men from very far away arrived at the stable. They had followed a bright new star that had come in the sky. They knew it was a sign that a king had been born. Then these very rich and important men knelt and offered gifts to the baby. Joseph and Mary were amazed. Then they remembered that Jesus was the Son of God and meant to be the Savior and Ruler of all men.

All that night a warm light must have shone from the stable. Overhead the star glistened to show the way to Bethlehem. The news of Jesus' birth brought great joy and hope to the people. Their Savior had come at last!

Although over two thousand years have passed, we still celebrate the birthday of Jesus when He was born in Bethlehem. And the amazing joy of that first Christmas still lives in our hearts.

# SECRET 19

## *Keep Communications Open*

Have you ever noticed that when you're busiest, your children want to talk? We need to understand from the beginning that communication is the key to our children's hearts. This begins when they're forming their first words. We must stop at inconvenient times and put aside our important adult thoughts and activities to listen and talk with our children.

Listening to and talking with your children, asking how their day was, and acting like it is the most interesting thing in the world to you is a key to a happy child. You open wide the lines of communication from the earliest age, so when they are teens it remains the easiest, most natural thing in the world just to keep talking to you. For Susannah it went into and through college (Dad had the $800 phone bills to prove it), and so it remains today. But you have to create that bridge between you and your children.

Drop Everything
When Your Children Want to Talk

The children were all in school, and I had spent the afternoon in an intense counseling situation. My friend was crying and confessing deep things. I looked at my watch; it was 3:15. "Lord, what should I do?"

So I told my friend, "Its 3:15, and the children will be home at 3:30. I think that we should pray together and set another appointment to finish this." We prayed, and I gave her a hug. I was helping her with her coat when I heard the squeak of the school bus brakes.

The front door burst open. "Mom, we're home!" It was Phillip and Stephen, my precious younger sons. My friend thanked me, greeted the boys, and left. I changed my hat from counselor to mother. This hat, in my opinion, looked the best on me. We made our way to the kitchen. As the boys pulled up their stools, I poured glasses of milk and passed out the cookies.

"Tell me. What happened at school?"

"Well, there was a fight on the bus...." So it went, the details of a busy day in kindergarten and third grade.

"What's the homework story?"

"We don't have much."

So I said, "In that case, you better hurry outside and play awhile to get out some of your energy. We'll do the little homework you have after dinner. Remember to change your shoes!" I shouted to the back of their heads as they tore out the back door across the back patio. I turned to begin dinner when the front door opened again.

"Mom!" It was Susannah. She was a sophomore in a special college preparatory program at the local high school. Now this one I needed to keep close communication with. When the Lord leads us to have our children in the secular school, the first priority is good communication.

"I'm here in the kitchen, honey, come on out."

She flopped her books on the counter. "What's for dinner, Mom?" And then she began to cry. I dropped everything, put my arms around her, and said, "Shall we make a cup of tea and go sit in the den?" Keeping communications open with her was far more important than anything else at this moment.

I've had moms come to me, in tears, talking about trying to establish communication with their teenagers. If open communication has not been a pattern from childhood, there is more work to be done, and more patience and endurance. Speak less, listen more, choose your issues carefully, and prioritize creating a safe place for your child to talk. Your most important communication line at this point is prayer.

Build a bridge that will be able to bear the traffic of the trauma that the years may bring. It's an open door to be always available, always ready to listen. Our children are all grown now, yet many weeks they all call just to chat. "Mom, I only have a few minutes. I'm about to pull into work. I just wanted to give you my love for the day." Or, "Mom, is Dad there? Tell him I need to talk to him."

"I will son, and I know he'll get right back to you as soon as he can."

"And Mom, pray for me. Bye, bye."

# SECRET 20

## *Make Reading Stories Fun!*

It is difficult to say how important reading was in our home. It began with soft books and a baby snuggled in the rocking chair, turning the pages over and over again. If they had a favorite one, they wanted to read it repeatedly. Then, as each grew, we read on Daddy's and my bed every evening. Some of our favorites included C.S. Lewis' *Narnia Chronicles*, George MacDonald's two *Curdie* books, and the *Little House on the Prairie* books by Laura Ingalls Wilder. But we also enjoyed missionary biographies. I think we read them all.

Then Daddy got the idea that we would enjoy Dickens, so he chose *David Copperfield*. Oh, dear, the children groaned when it was time to read. But we plowed through, Daddy determined to finish what we started. Outside the children's hearing, I said to Paul, "Darling, they are going to hate reading."

Paul said, "No, it's good for them." Oh, we were fine until Paul came forth with *David Copperfield*, Volume 2. At this point there was a Petrie rebellion, and even Daddy had to succumb. So we learned that not all books are for all ages!

### Read Some More!
### Read Some More!

"Hurry up Matt!" Susannah urged Matthew to wash the dishes more quickly. "Mom and Dad are waiting for us upstairs, and I want to find out what happens to Laura."

"Oh Susannah, you know full well she will be fine. But it is exciting to see how they are going to get through this long winter." In just a few moments, the kitchen was cleaned, and "bedleys" were finished (this was the nightly process for brushing teeth, washing hands and face, and getting into pajamas). Now here we were, spread across our bed, Paul with the book, me sitting beside them with my needlework in hand, Matthew tucked under Daddy's arm, and Susannah across the bottom of the bed with her coloring book and crayons. We were ready to be transported together to the prairies of North America, to the long cold winter, as Laura Ingalls Wilder told her story.

The time flew by and Dad said, "That's a good stopping place; we'll start here tomorrow."

"Oh, no!" A loud groan came from the children. A chant rose up, "Read some more! Read some more!"

Daddy closed the book with a sigh. It was always a good place to stop when he knew that they would be excited to see how tomorrow's adventure would unfold.

You can see how important reading together was in our family life. We had a television but hardly ever considered watching it. There may have been some special program now and then, but reading was our evening entertainment after homework, dinner, dishes, and everyone was ready for bed.

We read in the same spot all together. Matthew was able to curl under Daddy's arm. Susannah had to busy herself, so she colored. Later, when Phillip came along, we weren't sure if we could contain him. The book did have to be interesting with a bit of excitement. And Phillip always drew or colored. Stephen, like Matt, was a reader and a snuggler. Each one found his own spot on the bed, his own way of listening.

Reading together gave us wonderful shared experiences and, in many ways, helped prepare the children for life. We all had a good laugh when Susannah reported that she was the only student in her freshman English class who had already read *David Copperfield*. Her professor said, "I would like to meet your dad!"

# SECRET 21

## *Trust God when Children Make Foolish Choices*

We give our children the tools to live by. We instruct them lovingly and clearly. However, there are points when we have to let them go to make foolish choices. Paul instructed them about the fact that the Scripture says, "Foolishness is bound up in the heart of a child." The following story exemplifies this in our own children.

### Triple Dog Dare!

"I dare you to jump in!" It was Phillip speaking to his younger brother, Stephen.

"I can't jump in. Dad doesn't allow me to!"

"I double dog dare you!" The pressure was mounting. Stephen always did what his big brother told him. But oh, the water looked cold, and he knew he couldn't swim. But a double dog dare! The swirling water between the two reservoirs was always high under the bridge in the spring. The current made it even more exciting and frightening.

Jimmy, the neighbor boy, who had been silently watching to this point, couldn't take it anymore. "Stephen, your dad doesn't allow you to do that."

"*Triple* dog dare you!" Phillip shouted. With that, Stephen jumped fully dressed into the cold swirling current. "Oh, nuts," said Phillip, realizing for the first time that he was going to have to save him. He was quick and sure as he jumped into the swiftly moving water to save his little brother. He got ahold of him and pulled him out. Both were soaking wet and freezing cold. I imagine Stephen was crying by this time. "Don't cry," demanded his older brother, as they made their way to the house. Maybe they could get in and up to their rooms without anybody catching them. They took off their shoes at the back door and quietly opened the kitchen door.

Oh, no, mom was standing at the counter. "What have you done?" Now Stephen really began to cry as the story poured forth. "Go immediately into Daddy's office and let him see you and hear your story. Here's a towel to dry up the floor as you go." This was known in our family as the day Phillip got disciplined for saving Stephen from drowning! Oh, the adventures of the two little boys.

Father is faithful to allow foolishness to be clearly shown. That day both Phillip and Stephen saw clearly the problems with their foolish choices. And Father will also be faithful to guard them carefully.

Most parents would agree that the teens are the most difficult time for our children. It is important that we negotiate these times carefully and prayerfully. I remember when Susannah was 13, she announced to me that she was not going to be a Christian, that she didn't believe. I told her that was fine, she needed to do what she must, but just to remember that her not believing in the spiritual realm made it no less real. And to be aware that Satan believed in her. This is the point in time where children often decide not to walk with the Lord, and from that point on they go their own way.

It's important that we, as their parents, love them through this time and let our faith hold them securely with thanksgiving. As Elizabeth Elliot said so well; "Leave with God what only God can do. Only God can change the hearts of men." When our Matthew went through a period of wandering from the Lord, Paul said to me, "Rebecca, we must not judge him, but love him. And in the end, our love will be the bridge over which he will be able to return to the Lord."

# SECRET 22

## *Listen to Your Children*

It's almost impossible to set a regular time to be with each child. It would have to be the right moment. I think the important thing is to know your child. Each one is different, and as we grow in our knowledge—giving them room to change and keeping up with the changes—we prioritize hearing them, listening and valuing all that they have to say. It begins when they're little and discovering the world, though what they're saying isn't really new to us. But because it comes out of their little hearts and minds, it's a treasure to us. I believe each child knows when his words are valued.

I talked with Stephen last evening. He's now a young man, twenty-seven, and married with two little ones already. We laughed about the story of his running away from home. He added something I had forgotten. He said, "Daddy took Susannah and me into the living room, and we sat on the couch together, and he said, 'Now,

Stephen, tell Susannah all that you felt and everything that happened. Why did you run away?' As I talked and expressed my four-year-old heart, everybody really listened. I remember, even today, that feeling that I was important and what I had to say was valued."

## You Busy, Mom?

I was feeling the press of dinner preparations with guests coming that evening. I had in my mind the outline of the times that I needed in order to be done in time. Everything was in order, and I was moving along a little like a freight train, when in came my precious Susannah from school. Now, Susannah was never interested in the kitchen. Maybe I loved it so much myself I didn't give her room, and when I tried to include her she was too busy or just not interested. So I gave it up.

But that afternoon as she swung in through the kitchen with her books over her shoulder, she flung them on the counter and said, "You busy, Mom?" Now it was one of those moments. You know you can't set the time to talk with your teenage daughter. You've got to catch them in the moment when they want to talk.

"No, Baby," I lied. "What's on your mind?"

She sat on the kitchen stool and began to pour out her heart. There was conflict at school, and she was feeling the pressure of being the only virgin in her gang. We talked, and I shared again from my heart how proud I was of her and how the beauty of her heart and walk with Jesus was a powerful life-giving testimony whether her friends valued it today or not. It didn't matter. But, you know, ultimately I felt they would, and underneath wished they were like her.

The kettle boiled, and I made us each a cup of tea. We went over and sat on the little loveseat in front of the fireplace at the end of the kitchen to continue our conversation. It was a golden moment, a moment in which I was able to affirm a beautiful blossoming daughter. What a treasure she was for the kingdom of God.

Sometimes listening to our children means they need to change, and sometimes it means we do. Here is what happened with two of our sons.

### Music and the Heart

One time when Phillip was listening to music with questionable words and messages, Paul sat down and listened to a whole album with him. As he listened with him, Paul asked Phillip what the words said because he couldn't understand them. As Phillip told his dad the words, even he was a little shocked at the content. He'd never really paid attention to what the song was saying. They then discussed the meaning and background of those concepts.

Paul led a conversation about the obvious differences in values, and even morals, between what the Scriptures teach us and what the songs were representing. When Phillip understood what the musicians were relaying, he made the decision himself not to listen to them again, and to be sure that in the future he knew the message as well as the music.

Stephen also had a time when he was listening to music that Paul didn't like. It was Dream Theater: no lyrics, just instrumental. Paul objected to the music style so he sat down with Stephen and listened to the whole album in order to try to understand why he found it so compelling. He didn't end up loving it, but did find a place to understand why Stephen did.

In these events I think you can see that learning to value and listen to the words of each child is a process. It begins when our children are very small and continues for a lifetime.

# SECRET 23

## *Teach Your Children to Value Inner Qualities Instead of Outward Show*

In everyday conversation with our children, it's important they have woven into the fabric of their character that true value is inner life. This is a lesson that can be taught many times a day by example and by words affirming their actions, such as praising Phillip for being courageous and Stephen for being brave.

### Click, Click, Click, and Beauty on the Inside

Hurrying down the airport corridor toward gate six, I held Susannah's little chubby hand. The click, click, click of her black patent shoes echoed, and her red, pleated sailor dress swung with every click. My bags felt heavy and my feet hurt, but I couldn't help but be lifted by the chatter on my right side. "Mommy, where are all these people going? How does the airplane stay up in the air? When will we get to the gate?"

"Oh, there it is, Susannah, up ahead." I said with relief.

We made our way to our gate and found a seat. Oh, it felt good to get off my feet. "Now sweetheart, you stay right near Mommy." I was thankful to be traveling with just one little girl. She would be content to stay close by and entertain herself by talking to the other waiting passengers.

"And where are you going?" Susannah asked the older gentleman on the right.

"I'm going to Atlanta, the same as you." I opened my book, and her chatter dimmed in my consciousness as I lost myself in my story. Suddenly, I heard the gentleman say to Susannah, "My, you are such a pretty little girl!"

"Oh," she replied, "My mama says to be pretty on the outside is not so important. I must be beautiful on the inside."

The gentleman got a surprised look on his face and, with a chuckle, replied, "Your mama's right, and I'm sure that you are beautiful on the inside, too."

Each of our children is different. My mother always said with a twinkle in her eye, that she was amazed at how different five girls could be! It's important that we recognize those differences in our children. At the same time, we must always be teaching by word and example that we value every difference. They must learn that we as parents value their inside character more than the outside appearance.

# SECRET 24

## *Protect Your Children from Sibling Strife*

In every family with more than one child, there develop sibling rivalries and strife. These conflicts can be family-dividing and shattering, causing life-long pain and division. Recently a friend shared the story of a family conflict born out of the death of the father. The three children each demanded a certain part of the inheritance and were not satisfied with what the parent had allocated. The conflict continued. My friend who shared this story with me ended it in tears, saying they were now in the courts over details that were worthless in comparison to their relationship, which was shattered now, probably beyond healing.

My mother often said to us, "If I die, and you fight over the little bit of inheritance that will be, I will rise up from my grave and haunt you!" This story about Mama gave Paul and me this story to tell to our children, and we laughingly say the same thing to them. And though we're laughing, they know how serious it is. "We only have what Father gives us." We trust it is deeply ingrained in our children.

## Two Approaches to the Same Problem

Our children have always helped do the dishes every night after dinner, while Paul and I went upstairs to watch the news. We often heard mounting screaming coming from the kitchen.

One evening the volume rose, and then we heard banging and rolling on the floor as two little boys are apt to do. A full-blown fight had broken out in the kitchen. Paul went downstairs and separated them. This was happening more and more often, so we decided to create a new schedule that would involve taking turns.

One week Phillip cleared the table and washed the dishes while Stephen dried the dishes and put them away. They alternated responsibilities every week. Thus we provided a secure structure by separation, which in this situation seemed the best.

Another time we heard screaming and then pounding on the back door. It was Matt and Susannah—doing the dishes. Paul went down to find Matt alone and Susannah outside pounding on the locked back door. Matt said, "Dad, I had a choice. I either could throw her out or kill her."

Paul said, "I guess you made the right choice. However, I believe there is another one. In this situation, Paul brought Susannah in and sat the two of them down on the living room couch each to tell his and her horror story.

Then to their surprise he said, "Now Matthew, tell me what Susannah said." And to Susannah, "Now what did Matthew say?" Such contorted versions each heard from the other, but Paul helped each to hear the other until they were able to forgive and continue their job serving the family.

For us, these two approaches were examples of resolving sibling rivalries. In every family there are conflicts that arise between children. You have to protect your children from one another. This can be great training for life if handled properly.

# SECRET 25

# *Protect Your Children from Outside Pressures*

When a couple goes through a season of stress, pressure, or intensity, be prepared for conflict. These stresses include family pressures, such as financial strain, strain with in-laws, and conflict in the workplace. I remember as a child how happy my home was and how my mother provided a protected atmosphere for me in which I was able to grow.

### The Littlest Warrior

I remember clearly one example when there was extreme pressure in my mother's workplace caused by my uncle, who worked in the company with her. The stress between them had grown to a point that it spilled over into our family life. One day at the dinner table, Mother broke down and began to cry. The whole story came pouring out over my little heart. I can remember as well as if it were yesterday that fury towards my uncles rose up within me in determination to protect Momma. Later that day I marched up the long sidewalk to my uncle's front door. I rang the bell, and he answered. I remember confronting him in blind rage for his attack against my mother. I began to cry and ran blindly down the sidewalk home.

The next day he confronted Mother about sending her daughter to speak with him. She had no idea what he was talking about. She told the story afterwards of going through each of my four older sisters to find the one who had confronted Uncle John, and finally realizing it was me, her littlest warrior and defender. It made a funny family story, but it is painful for me even today.

Another example of outside pressures is given by Paul from when he began to travel and time pressures were great on him and the family.

### How Not to Be an Absentee Dad:
### A Word from Paul

At some point when our children were young, I realized that I had the potential of being an absentee Dad, even when I was home. I have a strong sense of responsibility that resulted in long hours at the office, or travelling, and carrying the responsibilities home with me. After getting home I was often on the phone or doing correspondence, and sometimes I was thinking about my responsibilities so that, though my body was home, my mind wasn't. I'm sure Rebecca spoke to me about it.

One day I made the decision to leave my responsibilities at the office, or at least outside the door, and not carry them in with me to my family. That was difficult for me, and took focus and discipline, but now, thirty years later, I'm so thankful. Our children grow up so quickly, and once they are gone from the home, the opportunities to really be with them, know them, and let them know us, are passed.

These are a few examples of outside stress. Each family will know what stresses you need to protect your children from. Their little hearts and minds are not yet equipped to carry an adult load. This is why it's so important that the couple communicate well between them, working through stressful problems in life, and why single parents must have another person with whom they communicate and share through difficulties. In this way we are able to protect our children from the things they are not yet equipped to carry.

# SECRET 26

# *Never Discipline in Anger*

Early on before we had children, the Lord gave us some clear outline for discipline. He said the most important thing was never to discipline them out of anger. We realized that if we disciplined out of anger, we were disciplining them for our sake and not theirs. If it felt good, it was wrong. So how do we get over wanting to kill them?

For me, I took the offender and sat them in a chair. "You sit here until I get over being mad. I'm going to be with the Lord."

Now that they are grown, we sometimes tell stories about those times in the chair. Susannah says, "They were the longest times of my life, waiting for Mom."

Paul tells the story of Phillip after receiving discipline. He was four years old. As Phillip turned to leave, he turned back to Paul and said, "Thank you, Dad."

And we laugh about Susannah saying to me one day, "You know, Mom, I'm never going to obey you if you don't give me stricter discipline than that."

"Well, thank you dear. We'll be sure to do that." And we did.

Early on Paul and I decided we would not discipline our children with our hands. We wanted our hands to be implements of love and affection.

### Three Times and More

Susannah was by far the strongest-willed of our children. Often discipline with her was an ongoing process. I remember one morning she would not obey me. I can't remember the specific details. But I had disciplined her three times and realized she was no closer to obeying. I knew Paul was in his office that morning. I gave him a call. "Baby, she dug her heels in, and she is no closer to obeying me than when I started. Do you have time to come home?"

What is it about a dad that carries so much authority? It almost makes me mad, yet I am thankful, so very thankful for it. The front door opened, and I could see by the look on Susannah's face that she was breaking. Paul walked into the room, lovingly disciplined her, and she said, "I'm sorry. I will obey."

Special note for single moms: I think in the area of discipline, more than any other, you need to have a pastor or friend with strong, loving leadership that the family all respect. It's important that this man be a part of your family life, one who knows your son or daughter and loves them. Ask the Lord to give you such a man. It's important, if it would be necessary for him to discipline your child, that he love him or her, and that they have a real relationship built on mutual trust. However, even if it's not a matter of needing help to discipline, you single moms must have someone you trust to whom you can go with questions and concerns.

—

# SECRET 27

# *Know Your Plan for Discipline Ahead of Time*

Knowing how discipline works in a family is important for parents as well as children. Children need to know what to expect. When we were first learning to discipline and train Matthew, Paul told me, "Rebecca, it is too important to me that our home be peaceful and orderly. I'm not willing to let this little boy control and dominate our home." It was a short sentence, but it would set the tone for a home that was dedicated to serving the Lord and His people. It was a statement that declared that our home would not be a child-centered home, let alone a child-ruled home.

It set the stage for our children to join us in serving all those who entered. Paul and I were committed to serving the body of Christ in and through our home. And now we were able to invite our children to join us in that service, a focus that would teach them to be servants for the rest of their lives.

Our discipline of the children had become quite a ritual. We prayed, then we disciplined, and then we prayed again. Often we finished with the child expressing what he or she had learned.

## Discipline Can't Be Rushed

I remember once I was in a hurry. (Have you ever noticed how they often disobey when you need to get out the door?). After the discipline, Phillip cried "No, no!" This was a very unusual response for him.

"What's the matter?" I asked.

"You forgot to pray," he said. Indeed I had. We prayed together to complete the discipline, knowing Phillip's heart had internalized how important the whole process was.

Also, it's always good to have a special place for discipline. We usually chose the bathroom in the interior of the house, if possible. Discipline is a private matter and we didn't feel that the neighbors needed to share in that intimate family moment.

It might seem like Phillip was disciplined more than the others. It certainly was not true. He was just more articulate about it on these notable occasions. Matthew was our first child. I hope we disciplined him correctly. It is a reality that we learn on our first children. We'd never been parents before. We read a book or two, and he was a very wild child.

One time I remember coming into the church to find Matthew walking across the back of the pews. He was a climber, climbing every tree and hollering for Dad to come get him. Paul would talk Matt down, helping him figure out where put his foot next for an assured descent to the ground. Paul knew that Matt would continue climbing, so he wanted to train him how to get out of what he'd gotten himself into. Oh, it was difficult to discipline Matthew. I used to say that I needed a lawyer to deal with him!

## Sitting in the Corner—
## the Silliest Thing!

Stephen is "our baby," and was by far the easiest child. He almost never needed to be disciplined. Once he came home from school with this story: "The teacher did the silliest thing today. She made me sit in the corner. It was fine with me. I didn't mind at all. Do you know why she did that?"

We laughed and explained to him that it was a form of punishment, and that he needed to figure out what he had done to displease his teacher. But, you see, Stephen was our last and we, at forty-two, were very easy-going

**parents. Susannah often said, "Mother, Matt and I would never have gotten away with that."**

Our plan and expression of discipline changed through the years according to the differing needs and ages of each child. Probably there were changes in Paul and me as we got older. I'm sure things that were so important when we were younger we saw now with a different focus and plan. One of our basic goals in discipline was that the children would hear our voice and obey.

Paul says it well in this way: "When the children were young, we held the reigns tightly, expecting quick and thorough responses from them to our requests or admonitions. We wanted our children to hear and obey the Father's voice in their adulthood. As they grew older, we would often include them in the decisions. We'd ask them what their best thought was about a situation, and listen to their requests if they wanted to do something other than what we proposed. This was a time of them learning values, reasoning, priorities, consequences—essentially wisdom and personal responsibility." But it was our love that always held them in obedience and relationship.

# SECRET 28

# *Tame Your Tongue*

As I've grown more in my knowledge of Him, I've realized that Father can enable me to do what I can't do myself and that Paul will often expand my borders, often to my chagrin.

### An Angry Fight

Paul and I sat in bed in a friend's guestroom, probably 1971. It was so long ago I can't even remember the subject of our discussion. At least, it began with discussion, but quickly rose to a very high-pitched argument. Paul was becoming autocratic (his back-up style as a young man). I grew more and more angry. I'll never forget that he got up at this point and went to the bathroom. When he returned I exploded. I said every mean and hateful word I could think of. I raged at him.

As I watched, I saw the impact on my husband. I had wounded him deeply. He withdrew. What else could he do in the face of such a tirade? I sat in silence. I had definitely won that round. But had I? That night the Lord helped me make a decision. I decided never to speak to my husband in that manner again. A battle won like that was not really won.

That event was truly a turning point for Paul and me. We both realized we needed to be careful with our communication with each other. We didn't want to harm each other, or harm our relationship. It was vital that we communicate honestly, even if that hurt. But we chose not to say harmful, accusatory things that would hurt the other, or create walls and distance between us that weren't easy to retrace. We wanted to protect one another in the midst of disagreements and to discover a process of arriving at conclusions without damaging each other. It was important to say what we felt while being careful to protect the other. We would get through the disagreement and would even come to a common understanding without damaging the one we love in the process.

The same principle applies in every area of family life. When conflict arises through disagreement, strife, or stress, it's of utmost importance that you remember to guard your tongue. Words once spoken can never be retrieved and can bring damage and hurt to the ones we love most. At the same time life is full of stress and conflict.

There's a measure of that in family living that is healthy for a child to experience. This enables them to be better equipped for life.

There is another kind of stress: "adult stress," conflict between husband and wife. Paul and I decided to shelter our children from this as much as possible. We agreed that this would be worked out in private, and as much as we could possibly do it, not in front of the children. The only time we found this impossible was in the car.

## Fighting Doesn't Mean Divorce

Paul's driving was always a source of tension for me. One day it was especially bad and broke out into real conflict between us. I found out later that in the back seat, Phillip had begun to cry and said to Susannah, "Does this mean Daddy and Mommy are going to get a divorce?" She laughingly assured him that it was nothing of the kind, that we were always secure.

When I heard this story later, I realized that we must have been pretty successful at shielding the children from most of our personal conflicts. I trust the children learned by our example the importance of guarding your tongue. We live in a time where divorce is easy, and we must learn to fight with a tamed tongue so as to guard the hearts of those we love, both husbands and children.

# SECRET 29

## *Pick Battles with Your Children Carefully*

Through the years we have learned the importance of choosing carefully our battles with the children. I remember the time we had been waiting with joy for my mother's visit to our first new home. We brought her home from the airport. As she walked in the back door, Matthew greeted her with, "I don't like you, Grandmother. I want you to go home." I was horrified! I was ready to jump on him.

But my mother said, "Wait, Rebecca, choose your battles wisely. He doesn't know me, and I'll bet you have had too many people through the house this week." I knew she was right, and the profound admonition became a foundation for our family. Choose your battles carefully.

Loving with Few Words

I was standing at the kitchen sink when Matt came in the back door, head down, walking past me and said, "Is Dad in the study?"

"Yes," I answered.

"I want to see him. I don't want to see you."

"Hmmmm," I thought. That certainly was a statement I hadn't heard before. I wondered what he might be cooking up. I found out later he wanted to get a motorcycle. He had saved his money and found the bike, but he needed his dad's approval. He knew at that point he would never get mine, so he didn't want to ask his mother. Is it possible that at the heart of that relationship stood our choice to approve him and his bike?

Matthew had already moved out of the house and lived in an apartment. When Matthew came that day and asked about the motorcycle, he was coming home drawn by love. He was living with young men who were not walking with the Lord, working at Pizza Hut, learning about life the hard way.

I remember the day that he decided it was time to leave. As he closed the door I cried and cried as Paul held me. He said to me, "Baby, we can't make him walk the way we would have him walk. He's got to find his own way.

**We've got to just love him with few words and essentially that love will draw him back to us and to the Lord."**

So that day when he asked his dad about the motorcycle was not the time to battle but to let him go and know that he would be well-covered in prayer.

The primary element of choosing your battles is faith. Sometimes there are days with our little ones that we could discipline them all day long. In choosing our battles we are realizing that we will deal with one area and leave all the rest in Father's hands. Ultimately it is He who must care for and order the lives of our children.

No matter what, you must always have faith for your children. In the process of writing of this book and discussing with each child his or her part, Susannah sent me this beautiful email: "No matter what happened, you just poured faith into any situation. Your faith 'fed' me countless times when I had none of my own. It is easier now, most days, for me to have that first reaction of faith, but that is because of what I learned from you. But for the teens and twenties, I so deeply needed the 'training wheels' of your faith to keep myself steady. I think your faith for my life is one of the greatest gifts you have given me."

I chose this story above about Matthew because I could begin as a little boy with his grandmother and end with an almost-grown man and his motorcycle. I could do the same with any of the other three children. With each one, Paul and I have had to choose our battles carefully many times. It's a joy now that they are grown to see the pattern emerging. I can see how many choices have been built on the choices before and undergirding all Father's faithful hand and heart and the beautiful result today of four lives and families walking closely in Father's hand, fulfilling their destiny in the Kingdom.

# SECRET 30

# Live Relationally and Lead Your Child to Christ

Ever since my early years in college, I have had a special place to have my quiet time, a time each morning when I might seek the Lord, study the Scripture, and listen for His voice for the day. Through the years I've sought a special place in the house with a view out to some green area. Sometimes it was just the top of a green tree but enough that I could call it "my greening place." So each morning the Lord found me in my special chair looking out at my greening place, saying, "Well, Lord, here I am, and I praise and thank You for Who You are."

Paul also had to have his special place in the house, although he has not been as determined as I to have a perfect view. When the children were young, we lived in a big white house with a lovely greening place across the back. Every morning Father found me in my wingback chair praising Him over my greening place. It wasn't long until the children realized when they woke up where they could find Daddy and Mommy. First they slipped quietly onto Paul's lap, snuggling under the afghan over his knees. There was no need to talk, just to be held close in Daddy's arms, and in the quiet Presence they would learn to love. A kiss on the cheek, and then they slipped down the stairs and into the den. Sure enough, curled up on the wingback chair, Bible on my lap, teacup in my hand, I drew them close for a good morning snuggle in the Lord's Presence.

That was the beginning of the day. Throughout the day in many situations—anxiety over school work, conflict with the neighbor's child, departure to school—at every opportunity we stopped, took a moment, and turned our eyes and hearts heavenward and lifted the situation into Father's hands. The children were learning without a word of instruction that Jesus loved them and cared about every detail. We rejoiced together over answered prayer.

### Discovering with Our Children that God is Everywhere

I remember once Stephen calling me to the backyard during my dinner preparations. "Mommy, you have to come right now. Come sit by the lake. Look at the sunset. It's just amazing." As we looked together, we praised the Lord for His goodness and love.

Suddenly, I said, "Son! Our dinner is going to burn!" With a quick kiss on the head, I was off to the house, but with such joy, realizing my little guy had touched the Lord.

Living this way—with love and the reality of God in everything we did—made it easy for each of the children one day to meet Him personally. It seemed the boys always slipped into Daddy's lap on a quiet morning, but I shall never forget the joy and privilege I felt when a pig-tailed little girl with sleepy eyes came and curled up in my lap.

We were quiet one morning, when suddenly Susannah said, "Mommy, God is everywhere. Does He live in your heart? Could He live in mine then?" And so we prayed, and she invited Jesus to come in and take the Lordship of her life. The sense of the Lord's Presence was overwhelming. I knew there had been a transaction taken place far beyond my understanding, and I think it was then that I knew, as never before, that the Hand of God was on my baby girl's life, and she would be fine and was set aside for His purpose on the earth.

We've had many parents come to us through the years asking the question, "How can I lead my child to Christ?" I trust from these stories you are able to see more readily that our children coming into the Kingdom of God is not just a simple prayer and decision at one time. It's a beautiful tapestry woven in the relationships of our family love for one another and for Him. Your children will learn to be hungry for God by seeing you hunger. I have eight precious grandchildren. Susannah's learned to keep three-year-old Marta in her bed with books until she is almost finished with her quiet time. Then she invites Marta to get her little children's Bible and come and sit at her Mama's feet to have her quiet time when Mama finishes hers.

Joy in the jumble of life is all about relationships—from beginning to end!

# Postscript and Acknowledgements

It's been my privilege to again work with Rebecca on this, her second book. What a journey over the decades it has been, of an unexpected friendship, as well as quite a few journeys across the ocean. When we sat together last autumn, every day for over two weeks, and daily asked the Lord for the release of His purposes in this book, He always came with His Presence and the words just seemed to tumble out of Rebecca. I had the joy to catch them and record them for you to read. Then came the hard part: editing and finding just the right words for the title and the best way to tell the family stories.

Thanks to Susannah the story began. Thanks to Sarah, wife of Stephen, countless grammar and punctuation mistakes were caught. Thanks to the rest of the Petrie family who have shared their thoughts and ideas. It's been a great journey together.

There are two other very important people to recognize, without whom this book would never have come to fruition. First, my loving husband, Bill, who not only lives with me but supports me in this task, and also does all the final production, a big job. Second, Steve Tyrell again offered his services to design and create the cover as well as give overall design advice. He is a jewel to work with, and we trust he will receive a great reward in heaven.

Paul and Rebecca Petrie are the two most amazing people I have known on earth; and now Rebecca is no longer on this earth and her real life has just begun. Their lives exemplify the love of Jesus for everyone who knows them. And their children are true reflections of that love too. Their grandchildren are very precious, sensitive, caring, loving children. I am so deeply grateful to be part of their lives and a recipient of their love, to catch some of their joy in the jumble of life together.


Dorothy Leal
Editor, but mostly just a grateful friend of Rebecca, whom I miss
Columbus, Ohio
December 2014

Please send all editorial comments and suggestions to:
dleal@pobox.com.